MANIFESTING
WEALTH
AS A BLACK WOMAN
A JOURNAL & WORKBOOK TO BUILD FINANCIAL ABUNDANCE

MS. T. LANE

MANIFESTING

WEALTH

AS A

BLACK WOMAN

A

JOURNAL & WORKBOOK TO

BUILD FINANCIAL ABUNDANCE

BY

MS. T. LANE

TABLE OF CONTENTS

Moore's Publishing

Certified Publisher

How to Use This Book

Congratulations on taking the first step toward manifesting wealth! This book is designed to shift your mindset and guide you through actionable steps to create the life of abundance you desire.

Each chapter provides powerful insights, but true transformation happens when you actively engage with the material. That's why you'll find dedicated journal pages at the end of each chapter to help you reflect, plan, and track your progress. These interactive sections are where you turn knowledge into action.

How to Get the Most Out of This Book

1. Read Each Chapter with Intention – Absorb the concepts, stories, and strategies shared in each section. Highlight key takeaways that resonate with you.

2. Complete the Journal Pages at the End of Each Chapter – Each chapter includes guided prompts, exercises, and

action steps tailored to the topic. These activities will help you apply what you've learned and make it personal.

3. Use the Affirmations Daily – Every chapter includes affirmations to reinforce positive wealth-building beliefs. Repeat them aloud, write them down, or integrate them into your daily routine.

4. Track Your Progress – The journal pages include goal-setting prompts, gratitude logs, and habit trackers to help you stay consistent. Progress happens over time; documenting your journey will help you see how far you've come.

5. Take Action – Manifestation isn't just about thinking—it's about doing. Use the exercises to take small, intentional steps toward your financial and personal goals.

6. Revisit and Reflect—This book is meant to be used, not just read. Review past chapters, update your journal entries, and refine your goals as you grow.

Why the Journal Pages Are Important

Manifestation works best when combined with action and self-reflection. Writing things down helps solidify intentions, uncover limiting beliefs, and track life shifts.

These journal pages will help you:

- Clarify Your Vision – Define what wealth means to you.

- Shift Your Mindset – Replace limiting beliefs with empowering truths.

- Take Inspired Action – Plan and execute steps toward financial freedom.

- Cultivate Gratitude – Stay grounded in appreciation as you grow.

Note From the Author

This book is your guide, but you are the creator of your wealth and success. Commit to this journey, be consistent with the exercises, and trust that every step you take will bring you closer to your dream life.

Remember:

"Wealth begins in the mind and manifests through consistent action."

Now, let's get started!

With love and abundance,

Ms. T. Lane

Published By:

Moore's Publishing House

41593 Winchester Rd. Ste. 200

Temecula CA 92590

Visit our website at www.moorespublishinghome.com

Cover Design by Nubian FX

Edited By: Khloe's Thoughts Editing

Printed in the United States of America

ISBN:979-8-9985250-1-8

eIBSN:979-8-9985250-0-1

DEDICATION

To every Black woman who has ever doubted her power, questioned her worth, or felt like abundance was out of reach— this book is for you.

To my mother, Teni Denise Moore (1964–2012), who always believed in me, and to my grandfather, Lee Vada Moore (1936–2008), whose wisdom and encouragement inspired me to dream bigger. To my grandmother, Gerlyn Moore (1938–2021), who taught me how to carry myself with grace, strength, and class. To my great-grandmother, Sally W. Shirley (1925–2012), who showed me that health and wisdom go hand in hand. To my aunt Maxine Mitchell (1943–2013), who taught me that class should always be showcased, and to Uncle Chester Mitchell (1945–2018), who taught me that being great is more than just creating good work— it's a matter of self-discipline.

And to my children, Triniti and Dillon—you are my greatest blessings and my ultimate motivation. Every dream I chase, and every goal I achieve is for you. May you always know your worth and understand that the world is yours to create.

This book is for the dreamers, the doers, the believers, and those daring to imagine a better future. May you manifest the wealth, freedom, and joy you deserve.

With love,

Ms. T. Lane

Preface

Wealth feels like a distant dream for so many of us—a reality reserved for others but not for us. As Black women, we often find ourselves navigating a world that wasn't built for our success, a world that demands resilience while withholding resources. But what if I told you that wealth isn't just about money? It starts with a shift in mindset, a commitment to growth, and the audacity to imagine more for yourself and your legacy.

This book is my gift to you—a blueprint for manifesting wealth, not just as a financial goal but as a way of life. It's a journey I know intimately because I've walked it myself. I wasn't born into wealth. Like many of you, I had to figure it out through trial and error and a relentless determination to break free from limitations.

My journey started at rock bottom. I was unemployed, driving for Uber and Instacart to make ends meet. I was also in the middle of a nasty custody battle, fighting to keep my family together while barely holding myself together. Life felt overwhelming, and the dream of abundance seemed impossible. But then I stumbled upon the concept of manifestation.

I immersed myself in books like *The Secret* by Rhonda Byrne and *Ask, and It Is Given* by Esther Hicks. I started practicing gratitude, repeating affirmations, and visualizing the life I wanted— even when the evidence said it was out of reach. Slowly, almost imperceptibly, things began to change. My circumstances didn't transform overnight, but my mindset did. And that shift set everything else into motion.

This book is about more than achieving financial success. It's about stepping into your power, rewriting your narrative, and creating a life of abundance on your terms. It's about building a legacy—not just for yourself but for the generations that follow.

I wrote *Manifesting Wealth as a Black Woman* because I know the power of a dream. I know what it means to imagine the impossible and then watch it come to life. I know what it feels like to break free from the barriers of doubt and fear to step boldly into the future you deserve.

This isn't just my story; it belongs to all of us. It's a call to action for every Black woman who has ever doubted her worth, questioned her potential, or wondered if wealth was within her reach.

So, let this be your starting point. Let this book be your guide, inspiration, and reminder that anything is possible when you believe, take action, and stay aligned with your vision.

Together, we'll break barriers, rewrite the rules, and manifest the wealth you were always meant to have. The journey starts here.

With love and determination,

Ms. T. Lane

Other Works By Ms. T. Lane

AVAILABLE AT MOORE'S PUBLISHING HOUSE

Introduction

Imagine a world where you wake up daily knowing you can live on your terms. In a world where your financial worries no longer weigh you down, you can pour your energy into the things that truly matter—your family, your passions, your legacy. That is the world I want for you.

As Black women, we've always been the backbone of our families and communities, often carrying the world's weight on our shoulders. But when it comes to wealth, we've been taught to settle for less, to scrape by, to accept that the cards are stacked against us. Society has conditioned us to believe that abundance is for others, not for us.

I'm here to tell you that those beliefs are lies.

Wealth is not just for the privileged or the lucky. It's not about being born into the right circumstances or catching a lucky break. Wealth is your birthright, and it begins with a decision to claim it, believe in it, and take intentional steps toward it.

This book is about redefining wealth on your terms. It's about moving beyond the stereotypes and barriers to embrace the power of manifestation, strategy, and community. It's about blending mindset shifts with practical actions to create a life that feels abundant, fulfilling, and uniquely yours.

I've walked this journey myself. I know what it feels like to start from nothing to battle self-doubt and wonder if wealth was even in the cards for me. But I also see the power of imagining more for yourself—of daring to dream, act, and persist even when the odds feel impossible.

This book isn't just a guide; it's a movement. It's a call to every Black woman to step into her power, believe in her worth, and manifest the wealth she deserves. Together, we'll explore:

- **How to redefine wealth** so it aligns with your values and vision.

- **How to shift your mindset** and break free from limiting beliefs.

- **How to take practical steps** toward building financial security and generational wealth.

- **How to leverage community, relationships, and rituals** to align with your goals.

By the end of this journey, you'll have the tools to manifest wealth and the confidence to claim it unapologetically.

This is your moment to rise, to dream bigger, and to build a life of abundance for yourself and the generations that follow. Wealth is more than money; it's freedom, empowerment, and the ability to live on your terms.

Let's get started.

With love and belief in your power,
Ms. T. Lane

Chapter 1: Defining Wealth for Black Women

What Does Wealth Mean to You?

What does wealth mean to you? For centuries, Black women have redefined resilience, strength, and creativity, yet too often, wealth-building feels out of reach. But what if I told you it doesn't have to be that way? What if the keys to abundance, prosperity, and financial freedom have been within you all along?

I'll never forget the period when everything seemed to fall apart. I was out of work, driving for Uber and Instacart to make ends meet, and in the middle of a nasty custody battle with my narcissistic ex-husband. I felt stuck and powerless, like the walls were closing in. But during that time, something unexpected happened—I stumbled across the book The Secret by Rhonda

Byrne. Intrigued, I followed it up with The Power and Ask and It Is Given by Esther Hicks.

These books introduced me to the concept of manifestation, and for the first time, I realized that I had more control over my life than I thought. I started doing the writing exercises, practicing positive affirmations, and visualizing the life I wanted, even though my current circumstances seemed impossible to overcome. Staying positive during the custody battle was no small feat— anxiety crept in constantly. But these practices gave me strength, clarity, and a sense of control in the chaos.

At first, it didn't feel like much was changing. The courts weren't ruling in my favor, and I felt defeated. But over time, I began to notice something remarkable. It was as if someone put my manifestations into place behind the scenes like tiles laid by a master contractor. I didn't fully understand it then, but every affirmation, visualization, and positive action I took was building a foundation for the life I'm living now.

Redefining Wealth

Wealth is so much more than money in the bank or material possessions. For Black women, it's about freedom to live on our terms, care for our families without worry, and create a legacy that uplifts our communities.

When I began practicing manifestation, I realized wealth wasn't just about finances. It was about reclaiming my peace of mind, finding joy in the small victories, and building a future where I could thrive. For me, wealth became:

• Financial stability: Moving beyond survival mode into security.

• Emotional freedom: Learning to stay calm and grounded, even in the courtroom.

• Legacy building: Creating opportunities that will empower my children.

• Personal fulfillment: Living authentically and joyfully, no matter the circumstances.

"Wealth isn't just about the numbers in your bank account; it's about the freedom to live life on your terms, the joy of passing on generational blessings, and the power to uplift your community."

Manifesting Wealth as a Revolutionary Act

Manifestation isn't just wishful thinking—it's an act of self-love and revolution. When I started using affirmations like "I am worthy of wealth" and visualizing the outcomes I wanted, it felt strange at first. After all, how could I claim abundance when I was barely making ends meet? But I stuck with it, and slowly, my mindset shifted.

Even when the court rulings weren't in my favor, I could feel a more profound sense of control over my emotions. I started seeing opportunities—tiny, unexpected wins I hadn't thought to ask for. These moments gave me hope and reminded me that manifestation works, even when you can't see the whole picture yet.

Here's your first mantra for this journey:

"I am worthy of wealth. I claim abundance in all areas of my life."

Take Action: Your First Steps to Manifest Wealth

Before we dive deeper, let's set the stage for your transformation. Manifesting isn't about doing everything at once but taking intentional steps, one at a time.

1. **Reflect**: Write down what wealth means to you. Is it freedom? Peace? A home for your family? Take your time to define it in your own words.

2. **Visualize**: Spend 5 minutes each day visualizing your wealthiest self. What are you doing? How do you feel? Who are you with? Let your imagination create a vivid picture of your future.

3. **Affirm**: Begin each morning by repeating this mantra:

   "I am a wealth magnet. Money flows to me with ease."

Closing Words

This is just the beginning. You've already made a decisive change by redefining wealth and taking these first steps. The road ahead will require commitment, but remember this: Every action you take is an investment in your abundant future. Together, we'll break barriers, shift mindsets, and claim the life you deserve.

"Are you ready to manifest wealth as a Black woman? Let's begin."

Journal Section: *Clarifying Your Vision of Wealth*

Reflection Prompts:

- What does wealth mean to you beyond money?

  _____

  _____

  _____

  _____

- Describe the ideal life you would live if financial limitations didn't exist.

  _____

  _____

  _____

  _____

- What financial habits or mindsets did you grow up with? Do they align with your vision of wealth today?

_____

_____

Exercise: *Your Personal Wealth Definition*

- Write your definition of wealth in **one powerful sentence.** Example: *"Wealth, to me, means freedom, security, and the ability to live life on my terms."*

_____

_____

_____

_____

Affirmations:

- *"I define wealth on my terms."*
- *"I am worthy of financial abundance."*

Chapter 2: Shifting Your Wealth Mindset

What if I told you that your thoughts can shape your reality? You've probably heard the saying, "Change your mind, change your life." It's not just a cliché—it's the truth. When it comes to wealth, everything starts with your mindset.

Honestly, I didn't believe it would work for me when I first started learning about manifestation. I was carrying decades of limiting beliefs about money—what it meant, who could have it, and whether I was worthy of it. But once I began to unpack those beliefs, something incredible happened: I started seeing possibilities where I once saw roadblocks.

This chapter will dig into those limiting beliefs and replace them with truths that empower you. Because before you can manifest wealth, you must believe you're worthy of it.

Understanding Limiting Beliefs About Wealth

Limiting beliefs are the stories we tell ourselves about why we can't have something. They're often rooted in our upbringing, cultural messages, and past experiences. Here are some common ones:

- "Money doesn't grow on trees."

- "Rich people are greedy."

- "I'll never make enough to get ahead."

- "I'm not good with money."

Does any of this sound familiar? I know it does for me. Growing up, I often heard things like, "We can't afford that," or "Money is the root of all evil." Those phrases shaped the way I thought about money for years. I didn't realize they blocked me from seeing wealth as something I could create and manage.

The truth is that limiting beliefs aren't facts. They're thoughts you've repeated so many times that they feel authentic. But the good news is, you can change them.

The Power of Your Thoughts

Here's a lesson I learned the hard way: your thoughts are like seeds. Whatever you plant in your mind—fear, doubt, or abundance—will grow.

When I started saying affirmations like, "I am a wealth magnet," I felt silly. But over time, repeating those words began to shift my energy. Instead of focusing on what I lacked, I started focusing on possibilities. And guess what? The opportunities began to appear.

Manifestation isn't magic; it's science. Your brain has something called the Reticular Activating System (RAS). It's like a filter that helps you notice what's important to you. When you focus on abundance, your brain starts looking for evidence to support it.

Identifying and Replacing Limiting Beliefs

Let's do some work to uncover your own limiting beliefs. Take a moment to reflect:

1. What phrases or ideas about money do you remember hearing growing up?

2. How do you feel when you think about wealth? Excited? Anxious? Unworthy?

Now, let's replace those beliefs with empowering truths:

- Limiting Belief: "I'll never make enough to get ahead."

- Truth: "I can create multiple income streams."

- Limiting Belief: "I'm not good with money."

- Truth: "I am learning how to manage money wisely."

- Limiting Belief: "Rich people are greedy."

- Truth: "Wealth gives me the ability to help others and make a difference."

Write down your own limiting beliefs and transform them into beliefs without a limit. Keep these new beliefs (truths)where you can see them daily—on your mirror, phone, or sticky notes on your desk.

The Role of Gratitude in Manifestation

Gratitude is one of the most powerful tools for shifting one's mindset. Focusing on what one already has creates space for more blessings to flow into one's life.

I started a gratitude journal during my most challenging days—when I was driving for Uber and Instacart and stressed about my custody battle. Each day, I wrote down three things I was grateful for, no matter how small. Some days, it was just having gas in my car or the smile of a stranger. But over time, those small moments of gratitude added up and shifted my perspective.

Here's a simple exercise:

1. Every morning, write down three things you're grateful for.

2. Before bed, reflect on one moment from the day that made you feel abundant.

Affirmations to Reprogram Your Mindset

Affirmations are a key part of shifting your mindset. They're not just words—declarations of who you are becoming. Start with these:

- "I am worthy of wealth and abundance."

- "I release all limiting beliefs about money."

- "I attract financial opportunities that align with my goals."

Take Action: Daily Practices to Shift Your Mindset

By the end of this chapter, I want you to take these three steps:

1. Identify Your Limiting Beliefs: Write down the thoughts that have held you back. Replace each one with an empowering truth.

2. Practice Gratitude: Start your daily gratitude journal today.

3. Repeat Affirmations: Choose one affirmation and say it aloud every morning and night.

Shifting your mindset is the first step to manifesting wealth. It's not always easy, and you may face moments of doubt. But remember this: every time you choose a positive thought over a limiting belief, you're rewiring your brain for success.

You can create the life you desire—one thought at a time. Let's keep building.

Journal Section: *Releasing Limiting Beliefs*

Reflection Prompts:

- What are three limiting beliefs you hold about money?

    Example: *"Money is hard to come by."*

    1._____

    2._____

    3._____

- Rewrite each of them into empowering truths. Example:
  "Money flows to me with ease."

    1._____

    2._____

    3._____

- How do you feel when you think about wealth? Do you associate it with struggle or possibility?

_____

_____

Exercise: *Wealth Mindset Shift*

- Write down three positive money affirmations and repeat them daily for 21 days.

  1._____

  2._____

  3._____

Affirmations:

- *"I release all limiting beliefs about money."*
- *"I am open to receiving wealth effortlessly."*

Chapter 3: Turning Intentions into Action

Manifesting wealth isn't just about thinking positively—it's about combining Belief with action. Many people get stuck in this. They focus on visualizing their desires but fail to take the necessary steps to align their actions with their intentions. Here's the truth: Manifestation works best when you meet the universe halfway.

I learned this lesson during one of the most challenging seasons of my life. After reading The Secret, I started visualizing a better life for myself. But it wasn't until I put those visions into action that the changes became real. Manifestation isn't passive—it's active, intentional, and influential.

This chapter will explore how to turn your intentions into actionable steps that move you closer to the wealth and abundance you desire.

The Power of Clarity: What Do You Want?

Before taking action, you need to know what you're working toward. Vague goals lead to ambiguous results. Take some time to clarify your wealth goals.

Here's an exercise to get started:

1. Write Down Your Goals: Be specific. Instead of saying, "I want to make more money," write, "I want to earn an additional $5,000 in the next six months through a new income stream."

2. Break It Down: Identify why this goal matters to you. Does it give you financial security? Does it fund a dream? Does it provide for your family? Connecting your goals to your "why" gives them purpose.

When I first started manifesting wealth, one of my goals was to create an extra $500 a month to cover basic needs without stress. I got specific about how I could achieve this, mapping out small, realistic steps that I could take. That clarity helped me stay focused, even on the hard days. This step sounds familiar, and that's because the workforce uses it. Instead of calling it manifestation, they label it S.M.A.R.T. goals. Sounds familiar? **S**pecific, **M**easurable, **A**chievable, **R**ealistic **T**imely. See, the science of psychology is everywhere. You just have to pay attention. My $ 500-a-month goal was a S.M.A.R.T. goal; businesses use this technique to motivate employees and increase productivity, and guess what? It works. You even get so good at achieving these goals that you never want to leave the company.

Aligning Your Actions with Your Desires

Manifestation isn't about sitting back and waiting for things to happen—it's about aligning your actions with your desires. Think of it this way: when you place an online order, you don't just sit by the door waiting. You track it, prepare for its arrival, and ensure you're ready to receive it. Manifestation works the same way.

One example of manifestation going wrong is a story I was watching on T.V. About an African American woman who was terrified that one day a man would come and break into her home and rape her. According to her, she had a feeling her entire life that this would happen. She mentioned that her feeling and premonition were so vivid that she knew what he would wear when it happened. She called this a premonition, but this was a manifestation in my mind. She was very clear on how this would happen and very detailed about it. For manifestation to work, you have to believe it honestly. Although this turned out to be more of her worst fears coming to life, it explains how manifestation works, whether good or bad. That's why it is so vital that we are careful with our thoughts and intentions. The woman from the television show didn't predict anything; she *manifested* it by thinking about it daily, feeling the feeling of terror and fear, and knowing and believing it would happen to her one day until it happened. We can learn from this story by practicing positive thinking, positive affirmations, and positive actions.

Here's how you can align your actions with your wealth goals:

- Start Where You Are: Use what you have. When I started driving for Uber and Instacart, I realized those jobs weren't just about surviving—they were opportunities to build discipline, save small amounts of money, and invest in myself.

- Take Consistent Steps: Small, consistent actions create momentum. Every step counts, whether budgeting, learning a new skill, or setting aside $20 weekly.

- Stay Open to Opportunities: Sometimes, wealth shows up unexpectedly. During my manifestation journey, I found opportunities where I never thought to look, like side gigs and freelance projects.

Building Multiple Streams of Income

One of the best ways to manifest wealth is to diversify your income. Relying on a single paycheck limits your opportunities, but creating multiple income streams opens the door to abundance. The options below are just those options. If these aren't for you, open your mind and consider how to increase your income. Even if those specific things don't work out, you will still see income coming from various places, like a check from a closed bank account, funds from an old 401k, or a resurfaced life insurance policy. We can't control how, when, or where the manifestation will appear, but we know it will eventually occur if we put it into the universe.

Here are some ideas to get started:

- Freelancing: Use your skills to offer writing, graphic design, or consulting services.

- Side Hustles: Look into opportunities like online tutoring, selling handmade products, or even monetizing a hobby.

- Investing: Start small by learning about stocks, real estate, or cryptocurrency. Apps like Acorns or Robinhood make investing easy, even with limited funds.

You could even write a book or an e-book, which I assist with. Whatever gets that side hustle started, do it!

When I started exploring additional income streams, I realized how many opportunities were within reach. The key was being willing to try, even when uncomfortable or unfamiliar.

Setting Up Systems for Success

To stay consistent, you need systems that keep you on track. Here's what worked for me:

1. Budgeting: Create a monthly budget to track your income and expenses. Knowing where your money goes gives you control.

2.   Automatic Savings: Set up automatic transfers to a savings account, even if it's just $10 a week. Small habits build significant results.

3.   Tracking Progress: Celebrate small wins. Did you save an extra $100 this month? That's a win!

The Role of Faith and Patience

One of the most complex parts of manifestation is trusting the process. Sometimes, I doubted whether my efforts worked, especially when results didn't show up immediately. But here's the thing: manifestation is like planting a seed. You don't dig it up daily to check if it's growing—you water it, give it sunlight, and trust it will bloom.

During my custody battle, there were moments when I felt like giving up. The courts weren't ruling in my favor, and my efforts weren't paying off. But looking back, I realize that every action I took—every affirmation, every step forward—laid the foundation for my abundant life.

Trust the process. Wealth takes time to grow, but with patience and persistence, it will come.

Affirmations for Action-Oriented Manifestation

- "I am capable of creating the life I desire."

- "Every step I take moves me closer to abundance."

- "Opportunities flow to me easily, and I am ready to receive them."

Take Action: Daily Practices to Manifest Wealth

Here's your assignment for this chapter:

1. Set a Clear Goal: Write down one specific wealth goal you want to achieve in the next three months.

2. Identify Three Actions: List three steps this week to move toward that goal.

3. Create a System: Whether it's budgeting, tracking progress, or saving consistently, set up one system to keep yourself accountable.

Closing Words

Manifesting wealth is more than dreaming—it's about taking bold, intentional actions that align with your desires. You don't need to have it all figured out today. Start small, stay consistent, and trust the process.

You are capable of building the life you've always imagined. Now, let's make it happen.

Journal Section: Aligning Goals with Action

Reflection Prompts:

- What is one wealth goal you want to achieve in the next **30 days**?

  1._____

- List three small actions you can take toward this goal. Example: *Set up a savings account, start a budget, and research investments.*

  1._____

  2._____

  3._____

- How will achieving this goal improve your life?

  _____

  _____

  _____

  _____

Exercise: *30-Day Wealth Action Plan*

- Write down your **goal, steps, and timeline.**

    Goal:_____

    Steps:_____

    _____

    _____

    Timeline:_____

    _____

    _____

	Wealth Visualization	Daily Affirmations	Journaling	Budget Tracking	Gratitude Practice	Action
1						
2						
3						
4						
5						
6						
7						
8						
9						
10						
11						
12						
13						
14						

- Use a **habit tracker** to check off actions taken toward your goal.

30-Day Wealth-Building Habit Tracker

Consistency is the key to manifestation! Use this habit tracker to stay accountable and track your progress each day. Check off each habit as you complete it, and watch how your small daily actions lead to significant results!

How to Use This Tracker:

1. Review the daily wealth-building habits below.
2. Each day, check off the habits you complete.
3. Reflect on your progress at the end of the 30 days and adjust as needed!

Reflection Questions:

- Which habit was the easiest to maintain?

  _____

- Which habit was the hardest to complete daily?

  _____

- How has tracking your progress helped shift your mindset about wealth?

  _____

- What changes will you make for the next 30 days?

  _____

Keep going! Your daily habits are building your wealthy future!

Affirmations:

- *"I take inspired action toward my wealth goals every day."*

- *"Every step I take brings me closer to abundance."*

Chapter 4: Building Financial Confidence

Money can be intimidating. For many, just hearing "budget" makes us cringe. But here's the truth: building financial confidence isn't about knowing everything—it's about taking small, empowering steps to understand and manage your money.

I've been there. I didn't grow up with a wealth blueprint. I avoided looking at my bank account for a long time because I didn't want to face the reality of my finances. But avoiding it didn't change the situation; it only worsened it.

When I finally decided to take control, it wasn't easy. I had to confront my fears, educate myself, and build new habits. But with each step, I felt more confident, capable, and empowered. And so will you.

Why Financial Confidence Matters

Financial confidence isn't just about numbers—it's about freedom. When you understand and control your money, you're no longer at the mercy of unexpected bills, bad credit, or financial stress.

It also helps you make smarter decisions:

- You can invest in yourself and your future.

- You can say no to opportunities that don't serve you.

- You can build a safety net that allows you to dream bigger.

Step 1: Know Your Numbers

The first step to financial confidence is understanding where you stand. It's time to face the facts without judgment or fear.

Here's how to get started:

1. **Check Your Accounts:** Review your bank accounts, credit card balances, and debts. Write everything down so you have a clear picture.

2. **Track Your Spending:** Track every dollar you spend for one month. Apps like Mint or Goodbudget can help, or you can use a simple notebook.

3. **Calculate Your Net Worth:** Subtract your total debts from your assets (savings, investments, etc.) to get a snapshot of your financial health.

When I first did this exercise, I was shocked by how much I spent on little things like coffee and fast food. But instead of beating myself up, I used that knowledge to make better choices.

Step 2: Create a Simple Budget

Budgeting doesn't have to be complicated or restrictive. Think of it as a plan for your money that helps you prioritize what matters most.

Use the **50/30/20** Rule as a starting point:

- **50% Needs:** Rent, utilities, groceries, transportation.

- **30% Wants:** Dining out, entertainment, hobbies.

- **20% Savings/Debt:** Build your emergency fund or pay down debts.

Pro Tip: Automate your savings so you don't have to consider it. Even $20 a week adds up over time.

Step 3: Repair and Build Your Credit

Credit is one of the most powerful tools for building wealth. If your credit isn't where you want it to be, don't worry—you can fix it.

Here's what to do:

1. Check Your Credit Report: Use free services like AnnualCreditReport.com to review your report for errors or issues.

2. Pay Down Debts: Focus on paying off high-interest debts first.

3. Build Positive Credit: Open a secured credit card or become an authorized user on someone else's card to build credit responsibly.

When I started focusing on my credit, it felt overwhelming. However, as I paid off small debts and improved my score, I was motivated to keep going.

There's also the option of a legal CPN. Yes, I said CPN, and I don't care what the internet says about them being illegal. They are not. You can use a CPN Credit Privacy Number instead of providing your SSN, which is unlawful for businesses to ask for. Once it becomes a majority and all the companies are doing it, it becomes a way of doing business. I can offer assistance with this as well. Just set up a consultation at https://moorespublishinghome.com/coaching-appointments/ola/services/legal-cpn-for-credit.

Whichever route you choose, get your credit together. It's essential to your overall success.

Step 4: Start an Emergency Fund

An emergency fund is a financial safety net that protects you from unexpected expenses. Aim to save at least three to six months of living expenses.

If that sounds like a lot, start small. Even $500 can make a big difference when life throws you a curveball.

Tip: Use high-yield savings accounts to grow your money faster. Navy Federal has the best rates that I've seen so far.

Step 5: Educate Yourself

The more you know about money, the more confident you'll feel. Start by reading books, taking online courses, or watching videos about personal finance.

Some great resources include:

- Secret the Finance Industry Don't Want You to Know About by me, Ms. T. Lane

- The Black Girl's Guide to Financial Freedom by Paris Woods.

- Personal finance blogs like The Budgetnista

I made it a habit to learn one new thing about money every week, whether it was watching a YouTube video about investing or reading an article about budgeting. Over time, those small lessons added up.

Affirmations for Financial Confidence

End this chapter with empowering affirmations to rewire your beliefs about money:

- "I am in control of my financial future."

- "I deserve to be financially secure."

- "Every day, I make choices that lead to abundance."

Take Action: Building Your Financial Confidence Today

1. Check Your Numbers: Review your accounts, track your spending, and calculate your net worth.

2. Set a Savings Goal: Decide how much you want to save this month and automate it.

3. Learn Something New: Choose one financial topic to explore this week, like credit repair or investing.

Closing Words

Building financial confidence is a journey, not a destination. It's about taking small, consistent steps that empower you to control your money and your future. You don't have to be perfect—you just have to start.

You are capable of mastering your finances and creating the wealth you deserve. Let's keep going!

Journal Section: *Mastering Your Money*

Reflection Prompts:

- How confident do you feel about managing money on a scale from 1-10?

  _____

- What's one financial skill you'd like to improve? Examples: *Budgeting, saving, investing.*

  _____

- What fears do you have around money, and how can you overcome them?

  _____

Exercise: *Money Check-In*

- List your current **income, expenses, and savings.**

Income:_____

Expenses:

Rent/Mortgage:_____

Car Payment:_____

Car Insurance:_____

Utility 1:_____

Utility 2:_____

Other:_____

Other:_____

Other:_____

- Create a simple **weekly budget** and track your spending.

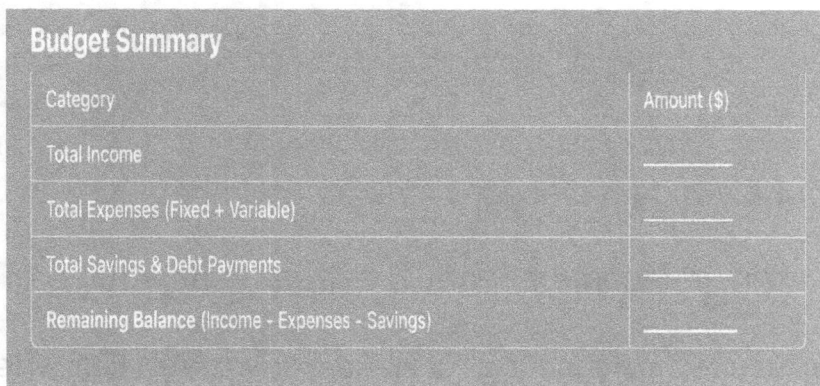

Budget Summary

Category	Amount ($)
Total Income	_____
Total Expenses (Fixed + Variable)	_____
Total Savings & Debt Payments	_____
Remaining Balance (Income - Expenses - Savings)	_____

Affirmations:

- *"I am in control of my financial future."*

- *"I am learning and growing in my wealth journey every day."*

Chapter 5: The Power of Multiple Streams of Income

One of the biggest lessons I've learned about wealth is this: relying on a single income stream is a trap. If one source of money dries up, you're left scrambling to make ends meet. But when you have multiple income streams, you create a safety net that allows you to thrive no matter what life throws.

When I was driving for Uber and Instacart, I realized I couldn't rely solely on those gigs to build the life I wanted. That's when I started exploring other ways to earn money. It wasn't easy, and I had to get creative, but every new income stream brought me closer to financial stability—and, eventually, abundance.

This chapter will explore why multiple income streams are essential and how to build them today.

Why Multiple Streams of Income Matter

Having multiple income streams isn't just about making more money—it's about creating financial security and freedom. Here's why it's so powerful:

1. Reduces Risk: If one income stream slows down, you still have others to rely on.

2. Accelerates Wealth-Building: Extra income allows you to save, invest, and grow your wealth faster.

3. Expands Opportunities: With more income, you can invest in education, start a business, or take risks that lead to greater rewards.

Step 1: Assess Your Skills and Interests

The best income streams are the ones that align with your skills, interests, and values. Start by asking yourself:

- What skills do I have that others might pay for? (e.g., writing, teaching, organizing)

- What hobbies or passions could I monetize? (e.g., baking, crafting, photography)

- What's a need in my community or network that I could fill?

When I started exploring additional income streams, I realized that my background in finance gave me a unique opportunity to help others. That eventually led to coaching, writing, and publishing—all new earning ways.

Step 2: Explore Income Stream Options

Here are some ideas to inspire you:

Active Income Streams (Time for Money)

1. Freelancing: Offer services like writing, graphic design, or virtual assistance.

2. Side Hustles: Start small businesses like event planning, tutoring, or cleaning services.

3.   Consulting or Coaching: Use your expertise to help others achieve their goals.

Passive Income Streams (Money That Works for You)

1.   Investing: Start with small investments in stocks, real estate, or funds.

2.   Selling Digital Products: Create ebooks, courses, or printables that you can sell repeatedly.

3.   Affiliate Marketing: Earn commissions by promoting products you love.

Pro Tip: Start with one or two achievable income streams, then expand as you gain confidence.

Step 3: Start Small, Think Big

You don't have to build multiple income streams overnight. Start with one idea and take small, consistent steps to grow it.

Here's an example:

•   Month 1: Research and plan your first income stream.

- Month 2: Start offering your product or service, even it's to a small audience.

- Month 3 and Beyond: Refine your process, expand your reach, and explore a second income stream.

I didn't have everything figured out when I started my publishing business, but I focused on learning, testing ideas, and staying consistent. Over time, that one stream grew into something much bigger.

Step 4: Leverage Technology

Technology makes it easier than ever to create and manage multiple income streams. Here are some tools to help:

- Platforms for Freelancing: Upwork, Fiverr, or TaskRabbit.

- E-commerce Sites: Etsy, Shopify, or Amazon for selling products.

- Investment Apps: Robinhood, Acorns, or Fundrise.

- Online Learning Platforms: Teachable or Udemy for selling courses.

Step 5: Keep Growing and Diversifying

Once you've built one or two income streams, start thinking about how to scale or diversify further. For example:

- Turn a side hustle into a full-fledged business.

- Reinvest earnings into investments or real estate.

- Collaborate with others to expand your reach.

Remember, building wealth is a journey. Each step you take builds momentum, bringing you closer to financial freedom.

Affirmations for Financial Growth

- "I am open to new opportunities to earn and grow."

- "Multiple streams of income flow to me with ease."

- "I have the skills and creativity to build wealth."

Take Action: Building Your First New Income Stream

1.   Choose One Idea: Pick one income stream you want to start.

2.   Set a Goal: Decide how much you want to earn from it in the next three months.

3.   Take the First Step: Whether researching, creating a profile, or reaching out to potential clients, take action today.

Closing Words

Building multiple income streams isn't just about money—it's about taking control of your financial future and creating opportunities for yourself and your family. Start small, stay consistent, and trust that every step will lead you closer to the abundant life you deserve.

Let's keep building.

Journal Section: Exploring New Income Sources

Reflection Prompts:

- What skills or talents do you have that could generate

  income?

  _____

- What's one income stream you could start this month?

  _____

- What's holding you back from pursuing new financial
  opportunities?

  _____

Exercise: *Income Brainstorming Map*

- Create a **list of potential income streams.**

  Potential Income Streams:

  _____ _____ _____

  _____ _____ _____

- Choose **one** and write the **first three steps** to make it happen.

1._____

1._____

2._____

3._____

Affirmations:

- *"I am open to new opportunities for financial growth."*

- *"Multiple streams of income flow to me effortlessly."*

Chapter 6: Manifesting Wealth Through Relationships

Wealth doesn't happen in isolation. One of my greatest lessons is that relationships are key to manifesting abundance. Whether it's a mentor who guides you, a friend who encourages you, or a network that opens doors, the people you surround yourself with can make all the difference in your wealth journey. This one has been tough for me to execute because I have trust issues with people. However, the few people I have let into my life have been essential to my growth. I learned that all friends must be a part of every aspect of your life. I have a friend that I send my books to when they are complete, and that's it. I have another friend with whom I discuss issues about my son's school. You can have friendships with many people, but they don't have to be in every aspect of your life.

During one of my most challenging seasons, I realized the value of relationships. While rebuilding my life, I leaned on a small circle of trusted people who believed in me, even when I struggled to believe in myself. Over time, I saw how connecting with the right people could provide emotional support and opportunities I hadn't considered.

This chapter will explore how to cultivate relationships that uplift, inspire, and support your wealth journey.

Why Relationships Are Key to Wealth

No one achieves wealth alone. Behind every successful person is a network of people who have contributed to their growth. Relationships provide:

1. Access to Opportunities: Networking can connect you to jobs, clients, and partnerships.

2. Support and Encouragement: A strong support system helps you stay motivated during tough times.

3.   Knowledge and Guidance: Mentors and peers can share valuable advice and insights.

Step 1: Build a Wealth Mindset Community

Surround yourself with people who inspire and challenge you to grow. That doesn't mean cutting off everyone in your life—it means being intentional about who you let influence your thoughts and actions.

Here's how to start:

- Identify Your Circle: Take inventory of the people in your life. Are they supportive of your goals, or do they hinder them?

- Seek Out Like-Minded Individuals: Join communities, clubs, or online groups focused on personal growth, finance, or entrepreneurship.

- Stay Connected: Regularly engage with people who share your vision, whether through coffee chats, Zoom calls, or social media.

Step 2: Find a Mentor

A good mentor can save you years of trial and error. Look for someone who has achieved the kind of success you aspire to and who is willing to share their knowledge.

Here's how to approach mentorship:

1. Be Clear About What You Need: Are you seeking career advice, financial guidance, or entrepreneurial insights?

2. Reach Out Respectfully: Send a thoughtful message or email explaining why you admire them and how their guidance could help you.

3. Offer Value in Return: Even if it's small, think of ways to contribute to the relationship, such as helping with a project or sharing your skills.

When I started my publishing journey, I reached out to people already successful in the industry. Their advice helped me avoid costly mistakes and gave me the confidence to take bold steps.

Step 3: Leverage Networking Opportunities

Networking isn't just about handing out business cards—it's about building genuine connections.

Here's how to make the most of networking:

- Be Authentic: Focus on building relationships, not just asking for favors.

- Share Your Vision: Let people know what you're working on and how they can support you.

- Follow Up: After meeting someone, send a quick thank-you note or message to stay connected.

Step 4: Strengthen Existing Relationships

Sometimes, the support you need is already around you.

Strengthen your current relationships by:

- Expressing Gratitude: Let the people in your life know you appreciate them.

- Offering Support: Be there for others; they'll likely support you in return.

- Collaborating: Work together on projects, ideas, or opportunities that benefit everyone involved.

Step 5: Avoid Toxic Relationships

Not everyone will support your journey, and that's okay. Learn to identify toxic relationships that drain your energy or undermine your confidence. Set boundaries and focus on the people who uplift and encourage you.

During my custody battle, I had to distance myself from people who brought negativity into my life. It wasn't easy, but it made space for healthier, more supportive connections.

Affirmations for Building Wealthy Relationships

- "I attract relationships that uplift and inspire me."

- "The people in my life support my goals and dreams."

- "I am open to connecting with those who align with my vision."

Take Action: Strengthening Your Wealth Network

1. Reach Out: Identify one person you admire and send them a message to start building a connection.

2. Join a Group: Find an online or local community focused on wealth-building or personal growth.

3. Strengthen a Relationship: Reach out to someone in your life and let them know how much you value their support

Closing Words

Wealth isn't just about money—it's about the relationships that help you grow, thrive, and achieve your dreams. By surrounding yourself with the right people, you'll manifest wealth and build a life rich in love, support, and opportunity.

You are not on this journey alone. Let's keep building together!

Journal Section: *Leveraging Connections for Wealth*

Reflection Prompts:

- Who in your life inspires you financially?

  _____

- How can you strengthen relationships that align with your wealth goals?

  _____

- What kind of financial support or mentorship would help you the most right now?

  _____

Exercise: *Networking & Mentorship Action Plan*

- Identify **three people** to connect with about wealth-building.

  1._____

  2._____

  3._____

- List **one action** to nurture each relationship (send a message, attend an event, etc.).

  _____

Affirmations:

- *"I attract relationships that support my financial growth."*

- *"My network is filled with thriving, abundant-minded individuals.*

Chapter 7: Overcoming Systemic Barriers to Wealth

As Black women, we often face challenges that are deeply rooted in systemic inequality. From wage gaps to limited access to resources, they didn't build those barriers overnight and won't disappear overnight either. But here's what I know to be true: We are resilient, resourceful, and robust beyond measure.

When I began my wealth journey, I realized that many of the obstacles I faced were not just personal but systemic. Instead of letting those barriers define me, I chose to find ways to rise above them. And so can you.

In this chapter, we'll explore the systemic challenges Black women face in wealth-building and develop strategies for overcoming them.

The Systemic Barriers Black Women Face

To build wealth, we must first understand the unique challenges we face. These include:

1. **The Wage Gap:** On average, Black women earn less than white men and women, even with similar qualifications.

2. **Access to Capital:** Black women are often denied loans or face higher interest rates when starting businesses or investing.

3. **Financial Literacy:** Systemic inequities in education mean many Black women lack access to financial knowledge early in life.

4. **Generational Wealth Gaps:** Many start from scratch without the safety nets or inheritances others may have.

Acknowledging these barriers isn't about accepting defeat—it's about understanding the playing field and changing the game.

Step 1: Shift Your Perspective

While systemic barriers are real, they don't define your potential. The first step to overcoming them is to shift your perspective from scarcity to abundance.

Here's how to start:

- Celebrate Small Wins: Each step forward, no matter how small, is progress.

- Focus on Your Power: Remember that you control your thoughts, actions, and decisions.

- Believe in Change: While the system may be unfair, countless Black women have broken through these barriers—and so can you.

Step 2: Close the Knowledge Gap

Education is a powerful tool for breaking down systemic barriers. The more you know about money, the more equipped you are to navigate the system.

Here's how to close the gap:

1. Learn About Personal Finance: To improve financial literacy, take courses, read books, and use online resources.

2. Seek Out Mentors: Connect with women who have successfully navigated similar challenges and learn from their experiences.

3. Join Financial Communities: Surround yourself with people focused on building wealth and sharing knowledge.

When I started my wealth journey, I immersed myself in learning everything I could about money—from budgeting to investing. That knowledge gave me the confidence to make smarter decisions and avoid common pitfalls.

Step 3: Advocate for Yourself

Advocating for yourself is essential whether negotiating a salary, applying for a loan, or seeking investment opportunities.

Here are some tips:

- Know Your Worth: Research industry standards to negotiate pay and benefits confidently.

- Be Prepared: When applying for loans or pitching an idea, come with a solid plan and the data to back it up.

- Practice Self-Advocacy: Rehearse what you'll say and how you'll present yourself in meaningful conversations.

I remember negotiating my first contract—it was nerve-wracking, but knowing my worth and being prepared helped me walk away with more than I initially thought possible.

Step 4: Build Collective Power

Change is faster and more impactful when we work together. By building and supporting networks of Black women, we can collectively break down barriers.

Here's how to build collective power:

- Support Black-Owned Businesses: Circulate wealth within the community by supporting Black entrepreneurs.

- Collaborate on Opportunities: Partner with other women on projects, investments, or businesses.

- Advocate for Change: Join organizations or movements that push for systemic reforms in pay equity, affordable housing, and access to capital.

Step 5: Embrace Resilience

Overcoming systemic barriers takes time, patience, and resilience. Although there will be setbacks, every challenge makes you stronger.

During my custody battle, I faced obstacles that felt impossible to overcome. But I kept reminding myself that resilience isn't about never falling—it's about getting back up every time. Resilience will help you push through systemic barriers to achieve your goals. My daily thoughts were that I knew this was not the end for me, and my dreams hadn't even started yet. I knew everything I had been dreaming of would be at my disposal once I got through that battle.

I know that hearing about my custody battle is getting a little redundant, but it affected me a great deal. Although it was one of the worst experiences of my life, it also forced me to learn and grow. I had just laid my mother to rest a few months before my divorce started, so dealing with that and the divorce sent me through a whirlwind of emotions.

Affirmations for Overcoming Barriers

- "I am powerful, capable, and unstoppable."

- "Systemic barriers do not define my potential."

- "I have the strength to overcome every challenge I face."

Take Action: Steps to Overcome Barriers

1. Identify a Barrier: Write down one systemic challenge you currently face.

2. Create a Plan: List three actionable steps to navigate or overcome this barrier.

3. Seek Support: Reach out to a mentor, friend, or organization that can help you on your journey.

Closing Words

Systemic barriers are real, but they are not insurmountable. You can create opportunities that defy the odds by educating yourself, advocating for your worth, and building collective power. Remember, every step you take is closer to the wealth and freedom you deserve.

You are not just building wealth for yourself—you are paving the way for future generations. Let's keep pushing forward.

Journal Section: *Navigating Challenges with Power*

Reflection Prompts:

- What is one systemic barrier that has affected your financial journey?

_____

- What steps can you take to work around or overcome this challenge?

  1._____

  2._____

  3._____

- What resources or support systems could help you move forward?

_____

Exercise: *Problem-Solving for Success*

- Identify **one financial obstacle** and write **three possible solutions.**

Obstacle:_____

Solution 1. _____

Solution 2._____

Solution 3._____

Affirmations:

- *"I am powerful and capable of overcoming any challenge."*

- *"I create my opportunities for success."*

Chapter 8: Faith, Gratitude, and Patience: The Foundations of Manifestation

Manifestation isn't a straight road. There will be twists, turns, delays, and moments of doubt. That's why faith, gratitude, and patience are essential to staying on track. They are the anchors that keep you steady when progress feels slow or invisible.

When I was in the middle of my custody battle and struggling to make ends meet, staying positive felt like a full-time job, the courts weren't ruling in my favor, and the life I envisioned for myself and my kids felt so far away. But instead of giving up, I leaned into faith, practiced gratitude for what I did have, and trusted that my efforts were setting something greater into motion. Looking back, I now see that those small acts of faith and gratitude were the foundation of my success.

The Role of Faith in Manifestation

Faith isn't just about religion—it's about believing in the unseen, trusting the process, and knowing that what you desire is already on its way.

Here's how faith fuels manifestation:

- It Keeps You Focused: Faith helps you stay committed to your vision, even when the results aren't immediate.

- It Reduces Fear: When you trust that things will work out, fear and anxiety lose their power over you.

- It Inspires Action: Faith gives you the courage to take bold steps toward your goals, knowing the universe will meet you halfway.

Practical Ways to Cultivate Faith

1.   **Visualize Your Future:** Spend a few minutes each day imagining your wealthiest, happiest self. See it, feel it, and believe it's already yours.

2.   **Speak It Into Existence:** Use affirmations to reinforce your Belief in your goals, such as "I trust the process of my wealth journey."

3.   **Keep a Faith Journal:** Write down moments when things worked out unexpectedly or when you overcame challenges. These reminders build your faith over time.

The Power of Gratitude

Gratitude shifts your focus from what's missing to what's already abundant in your life. It's a powerful signal to the universe that you're ready to receive more.

During my most challenging days, I started a simple gratitude practice. Each morning, I would write down three things I was grateful for. Some days, it was as essential as having food or a roof over my head. But even those tiny acknowledgments created a ripple effect, opening my eyes to the blessings I already had.

Here's why gratitude matters:

- **It Attracts More Abundance:** When you focus on what you're grateful for, you attract more.

- **It Reduces Stress:** Gratitude helps you stay present and calm, even in challenging times.

- **It Builds Resilience:** Recognizing your blessings strengthens you to keep moving forward.

Daily Gratitude Practice

1. **Morning Gratitude List:** Write down three things you're grateful for when you wake up.

2. **Gratitude Visualization:** Close your eyes and picture how your life will feel when you reach your goals.

3. **Gratitude Jar:** Write down small wins or blessings on slips of paper and place them in a jar. Read them at the end of the month to see how much abundance you've experienced.

The Importance of Patience

Manifestation takes time. Like planting a seed, you must trust that growth is happening even when you can't see it. Patience allows you to stay calm and persistent, knowing that the rewards will come when the time is right.

Here's how patience works:

- It Prevents Burnout: When you're patient, you don't rush or force outcomes, allowing for sustainable progress.

- It Encourages Reflection: Patience gives you the space to learn and grow from your journey.

- It Builds Trust: The more you practice patience, the more you trust the process—and yourself.

How to Cultivate Patience

1. **Focus on Small Wins:** Celebrate every step forward, no matter how small.

2. **Practice Mindfulness:** Stay present by focusing on your progress today rather than obsessing over the end goal.

3. **Reframe Delays:** Instead of seeing delays as setbacks, view them as opportunities to prepare for something even more remarkable.

Affirmations for Faith, Gratitude, and Patience

- "I trust the timing of my life."

- "I am grateful for all I have and all that is coming."

- "I am patient and persistent, knowing that my efforts will pay off."

Take Action: Strengthening Your Foundation

1. **Faith Exercise:** Spend five minutes visualizing your wealthiest self and write down how it feels to live that life.

2. **Gratitude Challenge:** For the next 30 days, write three things you're grateful for each day.

3. **Patience Practice:** Reflect on a time when patience paid off. Use that memory as a reminder to trust the process.

Closing Words

Faith, gratitude, and patience are the quiet forces that keep you aligned with your goals, even when the road gets tough. They remind you that progress is happening, even when you can't see it, and that your desired life is closer than you think.

Keep the faith, stay grateful, and be patient. Your wealth journey is unfolding beautifully—one step, one blessing, and one moment at a time.

Journal Section: *Strengthening Your Belief in Abundance*

Reflection Prompts:

- What are three things you're grateful for today?

    1._____

    2._____

    3._____

- How do you stay patient when things don't happen as fast as you'd like?

    _____

- Describe a moment when faith helped you achieve something great.

_____

_____

_____

Exercise: *Gratitude & Patience Journal*

- Write **three things you're grateful for** every day for the next **21 days.**

Affirmations:

- *"I trust the timing of my life."*

- *"I am grateful for the abundance I have and the wealth that is coming."*

Chapter 9: Wealth Rituals for Daily Practice

Success is built on the small, consistent actions we take daily. Creating wealth is no different. By incorporating simple rituals into your daily life, you stay aligned with your goals and train your mind and body to attract abundance naturally.

During my wealth journey, I discovered that the habits I practiced daily were just as important as the significant steps I took. Whether journaling my goals, repeating affirmations, or reviewing my finances, these small rituals kept me focused and motivated. In this chapter, I'll share the wealth rituals that have transformed my life and can transform yours, too.

Why Daily Rituals Matter

Wealth rituals are more than just tasks; they're intentional acts that reinforce one's Belief in one's goals and help one stay consistent.

Here's why they work:

1. They Build Momentum: Small actions add up over time, creating a snowball effect.

2. They Keep You Focused: Rituals help you avoid distractions and stay aligned with your vision.

3. They Signal Commitment: When you show up for your goals daily, you're telling the universe—and yourself— that you're serious about achieving them.

Wealth Rituals to Incorporate Into Your Day

1. Morning Visualization and Affirmations

Start your day by visualizing your wealthiest self. Close your eyes and picture your life as you've achieved your goals. What are you doing? How does it feel?

Follow this with affirmations that align with your vision:

- "I am a magnet for wealth and abundance."

- "I have everything I need to create the life I desire."

- "Opportunities flow to me effortlessly."

Time Needed: 5-10 minutes

2. Gratitude Journaling

Each morning or evening, write down three things you're grateful for. Gratitude shifts your focus from lack to abundance, helping you attract more of what you desire.

Example:

- I'm grateful for the roof over my head.

- I'm grateful for the people who support me.

- I'm grateful for the opportunities that are coming my way.

Time Needed: 5-10 minutes

3. Daily Goal Setting

Every morning, write down one financial goal you want to focus on for the day. It could be as simple as saving $5, learning something new about investing, or contacting a mentor.

Time Needed: 5 minutes

4. Money Review Ritual

Set aside time each evening to review your finances. Look at your budget, track your spending, and note any progress you've made toward your goals. It keeps you accountable and aware of your financial habits.

Time Needed: 10-15 minutes

5. Wealth Mantra Meditation

Take a few minutes to repeat your favorite wealth mantra while focusing on your breathing. It helps you stay calm, centered, and aligned with abundance.

Example Mantra:

- "I release all doubts and embrace financial success."

Time Needed: 5-10 minutes

6. Weekly Wealth Check-In

Once a week, take 30 minutes to reflect on your progress.

Celebrate your wins, identify areas for improvement, and set new

goals for the upcoming week.

Time Needed: 30 minutes

Creating a Ritual Schedule

To make these rituals a consistent part of your life, create a

schedule that works for you. Here's an example:

Morning Routine:

- Visualization and affirmations

- Gratitude journaling

- Daily goal setting

Evening Routine:

- Money review ritual

- Wealth mantra meditation

Weekly Routine:

- Wealth check-in

Customize this schedule to fit your lifestyle, and remember—it's better to start small and stay consistent than to aim for perfection.

Affirmations for Daily Alignment

End this chapter with affirmations to inspire readers to commit to their rituals:

- "I create habits that support my wealth and abundance."

- "My daily actions align with my highest goals."

- "Consistency is the key to my success."

Take Action: Building Your Rituals

1. **Choose One Ritual:** Start with one achievable ritual and commit to practicing it daily for a week.

2. **Set a Reminder:** Use your phone or a planner to schedule time for your ritual.

3. **Track Your Progress:** Reflect on how the ritual makes you feel and impacts your goals.

Closing Words

Wealth isn't just something you achieve—it's something you live daily. By incorporating these simple rituals into your routine, you'll stay aligned with your goals and create an abundant life.

Consistency is your superpower. Trust the process, commit to your rituals, and watch how minor actions create significant transformations.

Let's keep building

Journal Section: Creating Your Wealth Routine

Reflection Prompts:

- What daily rituals help you stay focused on abundance?

  _____

  _____

- How do you visualize your wealthiest self?

  _____

  _____

  _____

- What new habit can you commit to for the next 30 days?

  _____

Exercise: *30-Day Wealth Ritual Challenge*

- Choose **one** ritual to practice daily (meditation, affirmations, visualization, budgeting).

  Ritual:_____

- Use a **habit tracker** to stay consistent.

	Wealth Visualization	Daily Affirmations	Journaling	Budget Tracking	Gratitude Practice	Action
1						
2						
3						
4						
5						
6						
7						
8						
9						
10						
11						
12						
13						
14						

Affirmations:

- *"My daily habits align with my wealthy future."*
- *"I consistently take action to manifest abundance."*

Chapter 10: Manifesting Wealth for Generational Impact

Wealth is more than what you accumulate during your lifetime—it's about the impact you leave behind. As Black women, we often start from scratch, building wealth without the generational safety nets others may have. But what if you could break that cycle? What if you could create a legacy of abundance, empowerment, and opportunity for those who come after you?

I wasn't just thinking about myself when I began my wealth journey. I wanted to build something that would outlast me, give my children a head start, and inspire others in my community. Hence, I became an author. In this chapter, we'll explore how you can manifest wealth for today and future generationsy

Generational Wealth Matters

Generational wealth provides your family and community security, opportunity, and freedom. It breaks the cycle of starting over and gives future generations a foundation to build.

Here's why it's important:

1. **Breaks Cycles of Poverty:** Wealth passed down creates stability and reduces financial stress for your family.

2. **Empowers Future Generations:** With financial resources, your children and grandchildren can pursue education, entrepreneurship, and opportunities you may not have had.

3. **Strengthens Communities:** Wealth allows you to invest in your community, creating a ripple effect of abundance.

Step 1: Define Your Legacy

Creating generational wealth starts with a vision. What kind of legacy do you want to leave behind?

Ask yourself:

- What do I want my family to inherit financially, emotionally, and spiritually?

- How can I use my wealth to create opportunities for others?

- What values do I want to pass down along with my wealth?

Take a moment to write down your answers. Your legacy isn't just about money—it's about the values, lessons, and opportunities you create for those who follow.

Step 2: Build the Foundation

To leave a lasting legacy, you need a strong financial foundation.

Here's how to start:

1. Create an Estate Plan

An estate plan ensures that your assets get distributed according to your wishes. It includes:

- A Will: Specifies who inherits your assets.

- Life Insurance: Provides financial support for your family.

- A Trust: Protects your assets and helps avoid probate.

Pro Tip: Consult an estate planning attorney to ensure your plan is legally sound.

2. Save for Future Generations

Open accounts specifically for long-term growth:

- College Savings Accounts: Start a 529 plan for your children or grandchildren.

- Investment Accounts: Use long-term investments to grow wealth over time.

Step 3: Teach Financial Literacy

Passing down wealth isn't enough if the next generation doesn't know how to manage it. Equip your family with the knowledge and tools to build on what you've created.

Here's how:

- Talk About Money: Have open conversations about budgeting, saving, and investing.

- Lead by Example: Show your children how to make smart financial decisions.

- Provide Resources: Share books, courses, and tools that teach financial literacy.

When I began teaching my kids about money, I focused on simple lessons like saving a portion of their allowance and understanding the value of a dollar. Those small lessons laid the foundation for more significant financial conversations as they grew.

Step 4: Invest in Your Community

Building generational wealth isn't just about your family—it's also about uplifting others. When you invest in your community, you create opportunities for collective growth.

Ideas for community investment:

- Support Black-owned businesses.

- Donate to causes that align with your values.

- Mentor young people in your community.

Step 5: Embrace Long-Term Thinking

Generational wealth takes time to build, but every small step you take today makes a difference. Stay focused on the bigger picture, and trust your efforts will pay off in the long run.

Affirmations for Generational Wealth

- "I am building a legacy of abundance and opportunity."

- "My wealth will empower future generations."

- "I am creating a ripple effect of prosperity in my community."

Take Action: Start Building Your Legacy Today

1. Create a Will: Start outlining your estate plan.

2. Set Up a Savings or Investment Account: Open an account for long-term growth.

3. Teach One Financial Lesson: Share a simple money lesson with your family this week.

Closing Words

Manifesting wealth for generational impact is one of the most potent ways to create change. By intentionally building and sharing your wealth, you're not just making a better life for yourself—you're paving the way for future generations to thrive.

The seeds you plant today will grow into a legacy of abundance, empowerment, and opportunity. Let's keep building!

Journal Section: Building a Legacy

Reflection Prompts:

- What kind of financial legacy do you want to leave?

  _____

- How can you teach wealth principles to your children or family?

  _____

- What's one step you can take today to secure generational wealth?

  _____

Exercise: *Legacy Vision Plan*

- Write a **one-page letter** to your future family about the wealth you are building.

Affirmations:

- *"I am creating a lasting legacy of wealth and wisdom."*
- *"My financial success impacts generations to come."*

Chapter 11: Real-Life Stories of Wealth Manifestation

Sometimes, the most powerful motivation comes from hearing the stories of others who have walked a similar path. Manifesting wealth isn't just an abstract idea—it's a real, achievable journey that countless women have embarked on with incredible results.

In this chapter, I'll share some real-life examples, including mine, to show that manifesting wealth is possible for anyone willing to commit to the process.

Story 1: My Wealth Manifestation Journey

When I started my journey, I was at one of the lowest points in my life. Out of work, I relied on Uber and Instacart to make ends meet while navigating a nasty custody battle with my narcissistic ex-husband. I felt stuck, powerless, and uncertain about the future.

Then I discovered The Secret by Rhonda Byrne, which introduced me to manifestation. That book, along with The Power and Ask and Esther Hicks gives it, gave me the tools I needed to shift my mindset. I started practicing affirmations, journaling, and visualizing a better life.

At first, it didn't feel like much was changing. The court rulings weren't in my favor, and financial stress remained constant. But I stayed consistent. Behind the scenes, a higher power set my manifestations into motion. Years later, I can now see how every small step I took laid the foundation for my life today—one of freedom, abundance, and joy.

Story 2: The Entrepreneur Who Built Her Legacy

Meet Keisha, a single mom with a passion for baking. She dreamed of owning her bakery but didn't know where to start. With little savings and no business experience, she felt overwhelmed.

After reading about manifestation, Keisha decided to take action. She started visualizing her bakery, repeating affirmations like "I am a successful entrepreneur," and taking small steps, like selling cupcakes to her neighbors.

Fast-forward three years, and Keisha now owns a thriving bakery that employs six people and supports her family. She credits her success to faith, consistent action, and staying open to opportunities.

Story 3: The Professional Who Broke the Glass Ceiling

Monique was stuck in a corporate job where she felt undervalued and underpaid. She believed she deserved more but was afraid to ask for it.

After attending a workshop on wealth manifestation, Monique decided to change her approach. She started practicing affirmations like "I am worthy of financial abundance" and took actionable steps, like researching market salaries and preparing for a raise negotiation.

Not only did Monique secure a $15,000 raise, but she also landed a leadership position that aligned with her passion. Today, she mentors other women, teaching them to advocate for their worth.

Why These Stories Matter

These stories aren't about perfection—they're about persistence. Each woman faced challenges but stayed committed to their goals. Their journeys prove that wealth manifestation is not reserved for the lucky or the privileged—it's possible for you, too.

Your Story in the Making

Think of your life as a story that's still being written. What chapter are you in right now? What steps can you take to move closer to the wealth and abundance you desire today?

Affirmations for Inspiration

- "If they can do it, so can I."

- "I am creating my own success story."

- "My wealth journey is unfolding beautifully."

Journal Section: *Writing Your Own Wealth Story*

Reflection Prompts:

- Which story from this chapter resonated with you the most, and why?

_____

_____

_____

_____

_____

- Have you ever had an experience where manifestation worked in your life? Describe it in detail.

_____

_____

_____

- What lessons from these success stories can you apply to your own wealth journey?

_____

_____

_____

_____

_____

_____

Exercise: Write Your Own Wealth Story

Imagine yourself five years from now, living in full financial abundance. Write a one-page story detailing your life, how you feel, and what actions helped you get there. Be as descriptive as possible!

_____

_____

_____

_____

_____

_____

_____

_____

_____

_____

Affirmations:

- *"My success story is unfolding beautifully."*

- *"The wealth journeys of others inspire me, and I am creating my own."*

- *"Manifestation works for me, and I trust the process."*

Chapter 12: Your Wealth Journey Starts Now

You've come this far; it's time to take the next step. Manifesting wealth isn't just about reading or planning—it's about doing. The knowledge, tools, and rituals you've learned in this book are your foundation, but the power to create the life you want lies in your hands.

I know starting can feel overwhelming. I remember how I felt at the beginning of my journey—uncertain, nervous, and doubtful. But if there's one thing I've learned, it's this: The only way to fail is not to try.

Reflect on Your Journey

Take a moment to reflect on everything you've learned:

- You've redefined what wealth means to you.

- You've shifted your mindset and overcome limiting beliefs.

- You've learned practical strategies to build and sustain wealth.

Now, it's time to take action.

Your Next Steps

1. **Set Your First Goal:** Choose one specific wealth goal to focus on in the next 30 days. Write it down, break it into actionable steps, and commit to making progress daily.

2. **Create Your Rituals:** Use the wealth rituals from Chapter 9 to build a daily routine that aligns with your goals.

3. **Stay Consistent:** Remember, small, consistent actions lead to significant results.

A Final Word of Encouragement

You are more powerful than you know. Every step you take toward your goals—no matter how small—creates ripples of change. Wealth is not just about money—it's about freedom, empowerment, and the ability to live on your terms.

You have everything you need within you to manifest the life you've always dreamed of. Now is your time. Trust yourself and the process, and know that the best is yet to come

Affirmations for the Next Chapter of Your Life

- "I am ready to take the first step toward my wealth journey."

- "I have everything I need to succeed."

- "The universe supports my growth and abundance."

Closing Words

This is not the end of your journey—it's the beginning of something extraordinary. Go forward with confidence, courage, and the knowledge that you can create a legacy of wealth, abundance, and impact.

Your wealth journey starts now. Let's make it happen.

Journal Section: *Committing to the Process*

Reflection Prompts:

- What are three specific actions you will take starting today to manifest wealth?

  1._____

  2._____

  3._____

- What challenges do you anticipate, and how will you overcome them?

  _____

  _____

  _____

  _____

  _____

- How do you feel now compared to when you started this book? What mindset shifts have occurred?

  _____

  _____

  _____

  _____

Exercise: Your Wealth Commitment Letter

Write a letter to yourself committing to your wealth journey. Include your intentions, the habits you will maintain, and words of encouragement for yourself when challenges arise. Sign and date it as a declaration of your commitment.

_____

_____

_____

_____

_____

_____

_____

_____

_____

_____

_____

_____

Affirmations:

- *"I am ready to take bold action toward my wealth goals."*
- *"Every step I take is leading me toward abundance."*
- *"My financial success is inevitable."*

Final Reflection & Vision Board Space

- **Final Journal Prompt:** *"What has changed your mindset and habits since starting this book?"*

  _____

  _____

- **Create Your Vision Board:** Use a blank page to draw, paste images, or write about your wealth goals.

VISION BOARD

Conclusion

Sis, everything I've shared in this book isn't just theory—it's the daily roadmap. When I wake up, I first meditate for 15 to 35 minutes. Some days, when I need to focus on gratitude, I commit to a 21-day gratitude meditation. Other times, I dive into a 21-day manifestation-guided meditation to stay aligned with the life I'm building. I switch them up because balance is key—gratitude keeps me grounded, while manifestation keeps me reaching.

At night, I fall asleep to a guided meditation that focuses on the subconscious. It's like planting seeds while I rest, ensuring that my mind always works toward my desired life. Every day, I journal. If something doesn't go how I want, I don't give it power by writing it down—I simply imagine it going how I want it to.

Here's the thing: you have to play games with your mind to escape the limitations of this matrix. The mind is powerful, but it can be unruly. To grow, you have to use your imagination to manifest the life you want. Without imagination, there is no growth.

I marvel at the world around me—how freeways are built, skyscrapers touch the sky, and airplanes defy gravity. All of these things started as someone's wild imagination. It reminds me of a joke I once heard from the comedian Chris Tucker. He said something like, "The person who invented the telephone had to be crazy…to sit up and say, 'I want to talk to someone who isn't even here.'" Crazy, right? But it's true. Imagining something that doesn't exist sounds crazy—until it becomes reality. Then they call you a genius.

First, they'll say you're crazy. Then, they'll tell you're brilliant. So, no matter how crazy it sounds, imagine it, dream it, manifest it—because anything is possible.

Happy Manifesting, sis. I can't wait to see what you've created.

With love,

Ms. T. Lane

Leave a Review & Share Your Journey!

Sis, your voice matters! If *Manifesting Wealth as a Black Woman: A Journal & Workbook to Build Financial Abundance* has helped you shift your mindset, take action, or step into your power, I'd love to hear about it!

Why Your Review Matters:

It helps other Black women discover this book and start their wealth journey.

Encourages more books and resources that support Black women's financial empowerment.

Supports my mission to help more women like YOU break barriers and build abundance!

How to Leave a Review on Amazon:

1. **Go to Amazon,** where you purchased the book.
2. Scroll down to the **"Write a Customer Review"** section.
3. Share your thoughts! What did you love? How did it impact your journey?
4. Click **Submit**—and just like that, you've helped another Black woman start her wealth journey!

✏️ **Want to Share Your Story?**

Tag me on social media @ moores_publishing and use

#ManifestingWealthBlackWomen so I can celebrate your progress with you!

Your words have power, and your review has a ripple effect of wealth-building energy. Thank you for sharing this journey with me!